SUPER EASY SONGBOOK

Disney

FROZEN COLLECTION

Disney Characters and Artwork © Disney

ISBN 978-1-5400-8464-4

Hal•Leonard®

Visit Hal Leonard Online at
www.halleonard.com

Contact us:
Hal Leonard
7777 West Bluemound Road
Milwaukee, WI 53213
Email: info@halleonard.com

In Europe, contact:
Hal Leonard Europe Limited
42 Wigmore Street
Marylebone, London, W1U 2RN
Email: info@halleonardeurope.com

In Australia, contact:
Hal Leonard Australia Pty. Ltd.
4 Lentara Court
Cheltenham, Victoria, 3192 Australia
Email: info@halleonard.com.au

Welcome to the *Super Easy Songbook* series!

This unique collection will help you play your favorite songs quickly and easily. Here's how it works:

- Play the simplified melody with your right hand. Letter names appear inside each note to assist you.

- There are no key signatures to worry about! If a sharp ♯ or flat ♭ is needed, it is shown beside the note each time.

- There are no page turns, so your hands never have to leave the keyboard.

- If two notes are connected by a tie ⌣, hold the first note for the combined number of beats. (The second note does not show a letter name since it is not re-struck.)

- Add basic chords with your left hand using the provided keyboard diagrams. Chord voicings have been carefully chosen to minimize hand movement.

- The left-hand rhythm is up to you, and chord notes can be played together or separately. Be creative!

- If the chords sound muddy, move your left hand an octave* higher. If this gets in the way of playing the melody, move your right hand an octave higher as well.

> *An octave spans eight notes. If your starting note is C, the next C to the right is an octave higher.*

———————————————— ALSO AVAILABLE ————————————————

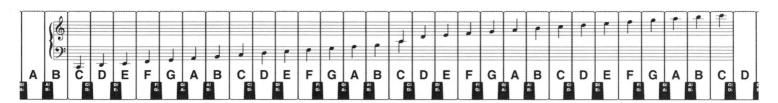

Hal Leonard Student Keyboard Guide HL00296039

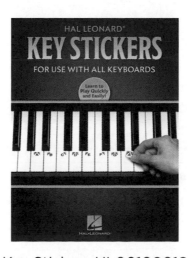

Key Stickers HL00100016

Do You Want to Build a Snowman?

from Disney's *FROZEN*

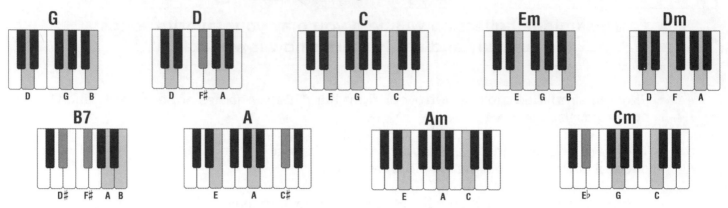

Music and Lyrics by Kristen Anderson-Lopez
and Robert Lopez

Brightly
(no chord)

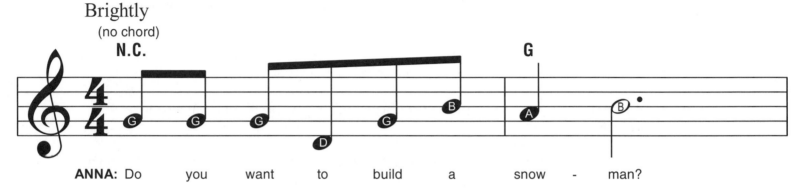

ANNA: Do you want to build a snow - man?

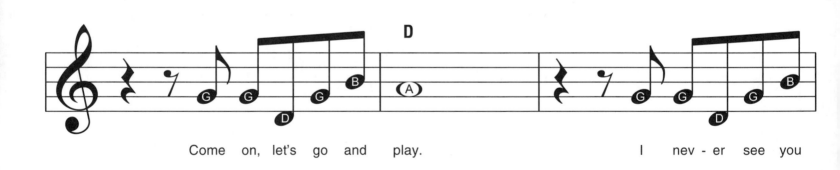

Come on, let's go and play. I nev - er see you

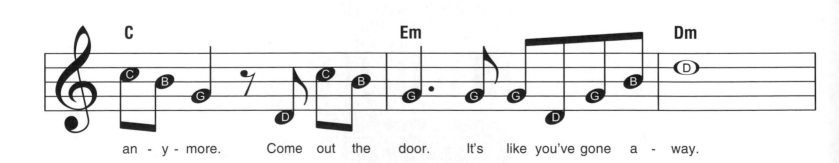

an - y - more. Come out the door. It's like you've gone a - way.

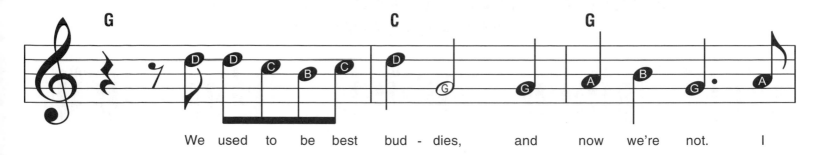

We used to be best bud - dies, and now we're not. I

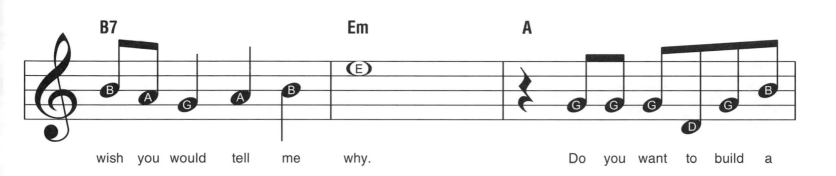

wish you would tell me why. Do you want to build a

snow - man? It does - n't have to be a

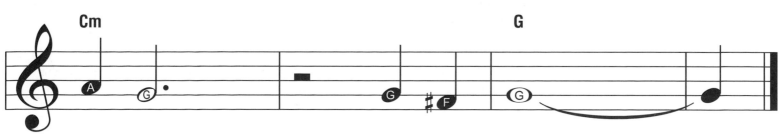

snow - man. **ELSA:** *Go away, Anna.* **ANNA:** O - kay, bye.

For the First Time in Forever
from Disney's *FROZEN*

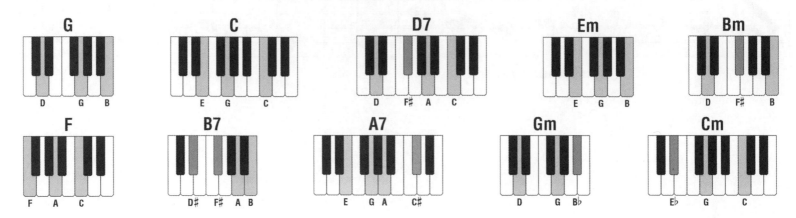

Music and Lyrics by Kristen Anderson-Lopez
and Robert Lopez

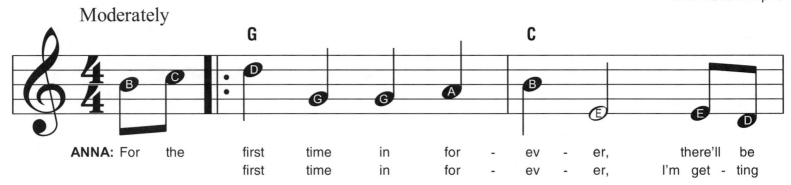

Moderately

ANNA: For the first time in for - ev - er, there'll be
first time in for - ev - er, I'm get - ting

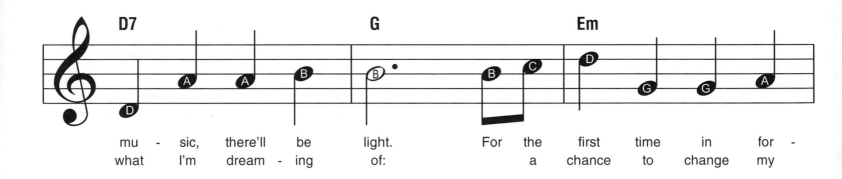

mu - sic, there'll be light. For the first time in for -
what I'm dream - ing of: a chance to change my

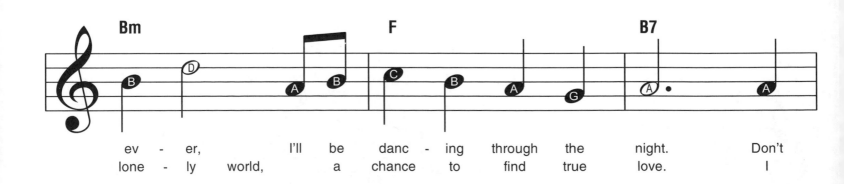

ev - er, I'll be danc - ing through the night. Don't
lone - ly world, a chance to find true love. I

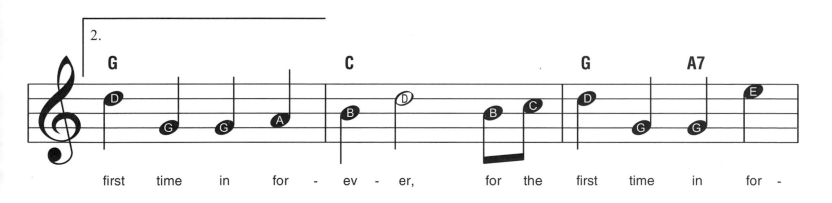

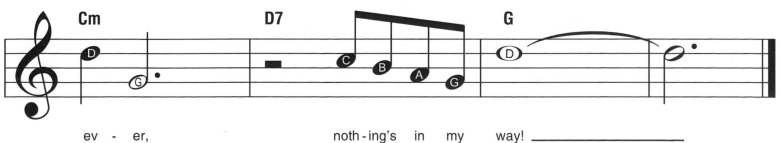

Love Is an Open Door
from Disney's FROZEN

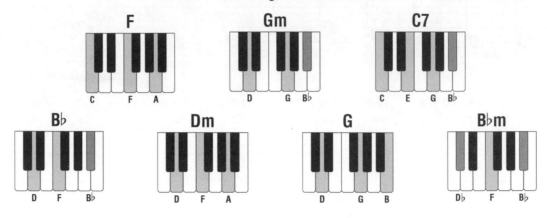

Music and Lyrics by Kristen Anderson-Lopez
and Robert Lopez

Moderately fast

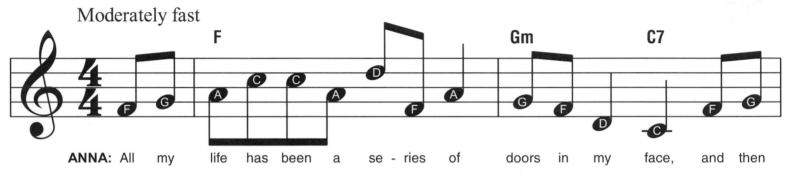

ANNA: All my life has been a se - ries of doors in my face, and then

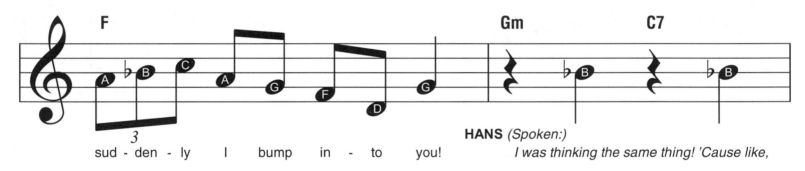

sud - den - ly I bump in - to you!

HANS (Spoken:)
I was thinking the same thing! 'Cause like,

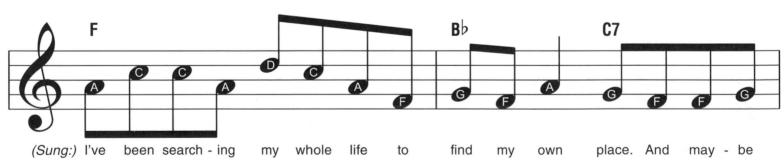

(Sung:) I've been search - ing my whole life to find my own place. And may - be

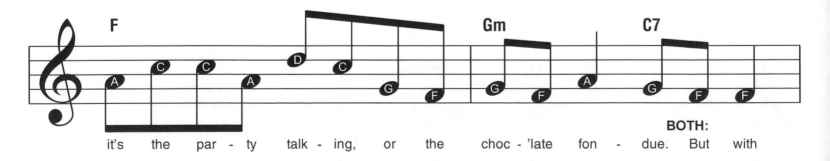

it's the par - ty talk - ing, or the choc - 'late fon - due. But with

BOTH:

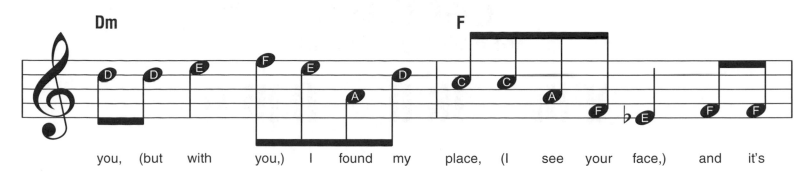

you, (but with you,) I found my place, (I see your face,) and it's

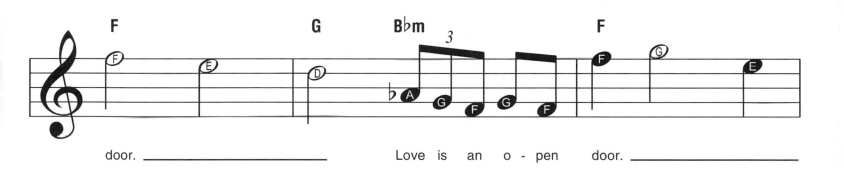

noth - ing like I've ev - er known be - fore. Love is an o - pen

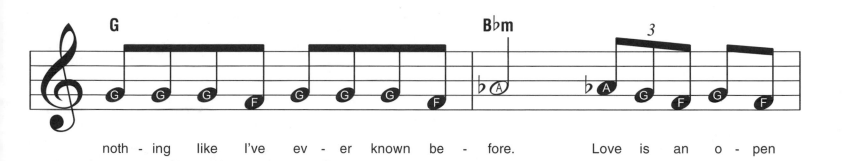

door. _____ Love is an o - pen door. _____

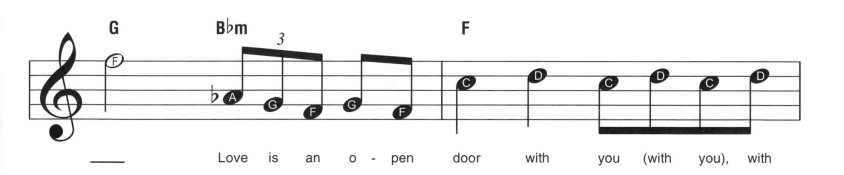

_____ Love is an o - pen door with you (with you), with

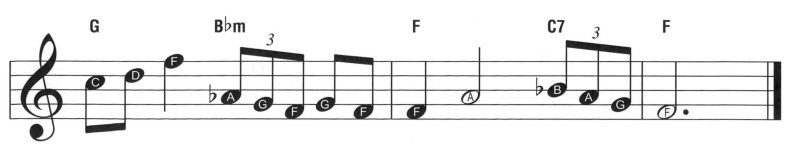

you (with you)! Love is an o - pen door. _____

Let It Go
from Disney's *FROZEN*

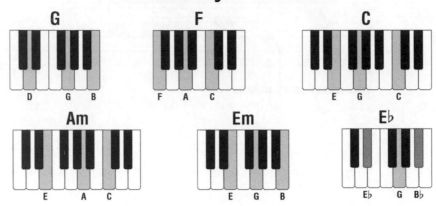

Music and Lyrics by Kristen Anderson-Lopez
and Robert Lopez

Flowing

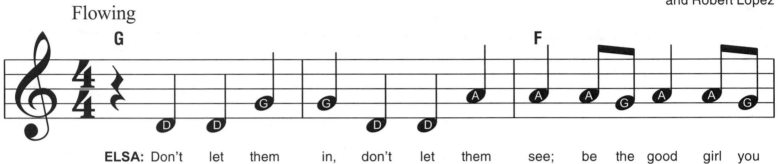

ELSA: Don't let them in, don't let them see; be the good girl you

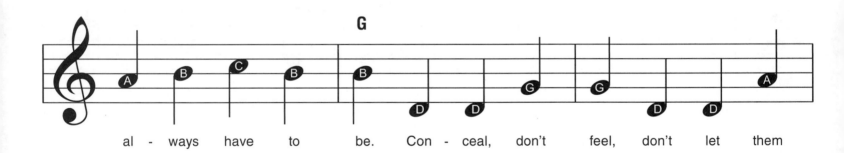

al - ways have to be. Con - ceal, don't feel, don't let them

know... _____ Well, now they know. _____

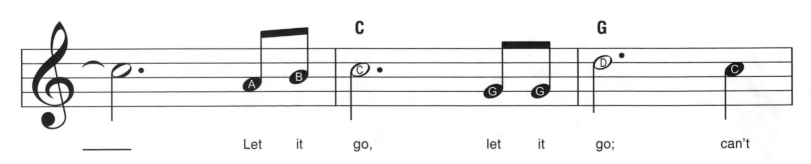

_____ Let it go, let it go; can't

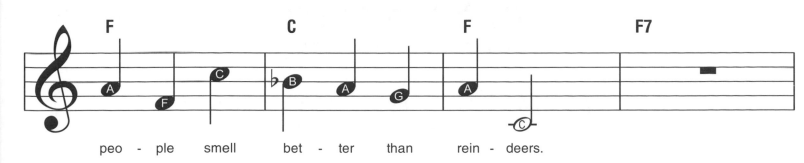

peo - ple smell bet - ter than rein - deers.

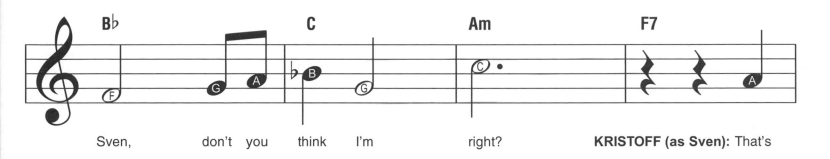

Sven, don't you think I'm right? **KRISTOFF (as Sven):** That's

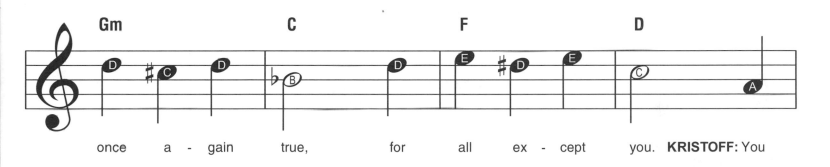

once a - gain true, for all ex - cept you. **KRISTOFF:** You

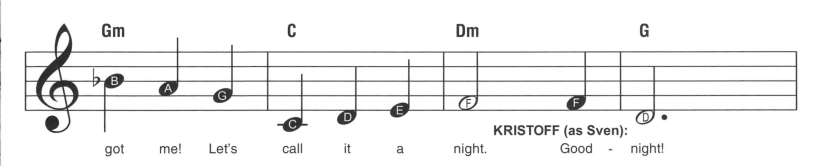

got me! Let's call it a night. Good - night! **KRISTOFF (as Sven):**

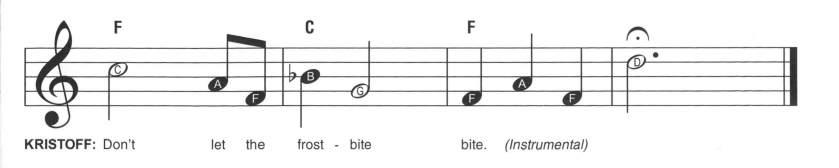

KRISTOFF: Don't let the frost - bite bite. *(Instrumental)*

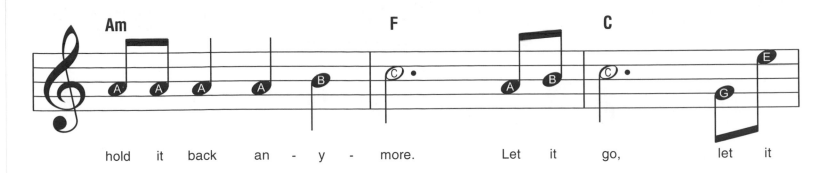

hold it back an - y - more. Let it go, let it

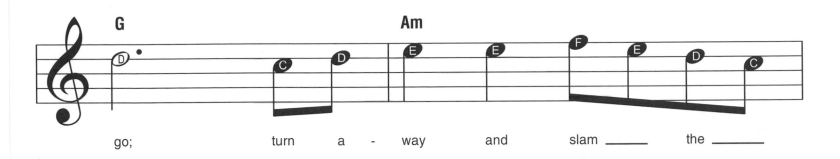

go; turn a - way and slam _____ the _____

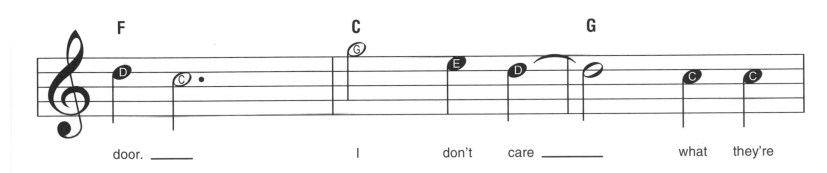

door. _____ I don't care _____ what they're

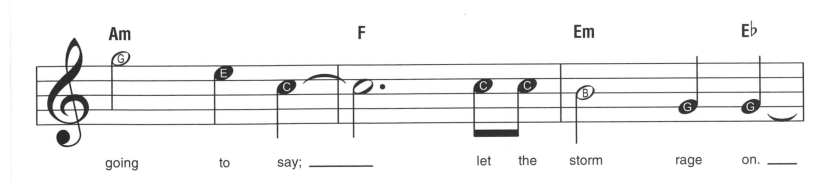

going to say; _____ let the storm rage on. _____

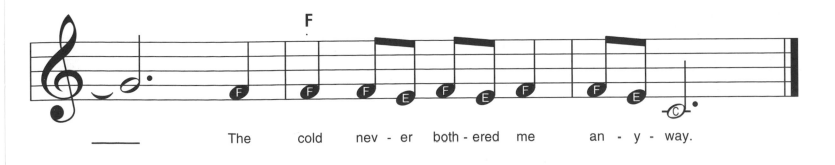

_____ The cold nev - er both - ered me an - y - way.

Reindeer(s) Are Better Than People
from Disney's FROZEN

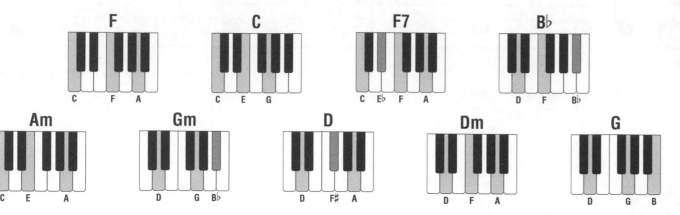

Music and Lyrics by Kristen Anderson-Lopez
and Robert Lopez

Freely

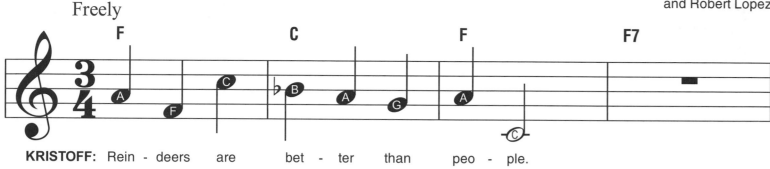

KRISTOFF: Rein - deers are bet - ter than peo - ple.

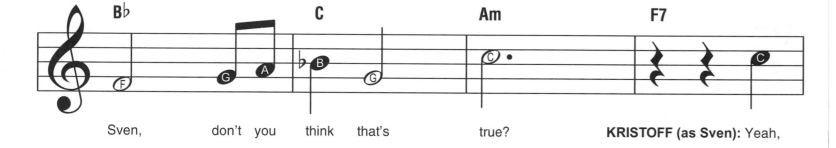

Sven, don't you think that's true? **KRISTOFF (as Sven):** Yeah,

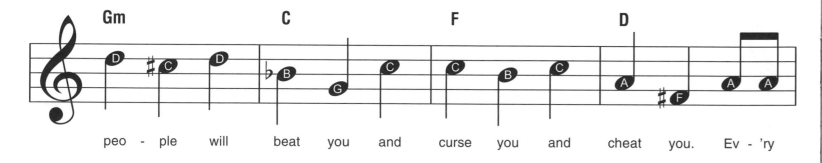

peo - ple will beat you and curse you and cheat you. Ev - 'ry

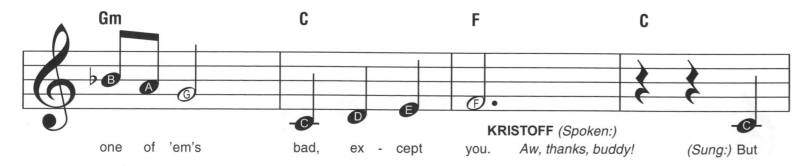

one of 'em's bad, ex - cept you. KRISTOFF (Spoken): Aw, thanks, buddy! (Sung:) But

In Summer
from Disney's FROZEN

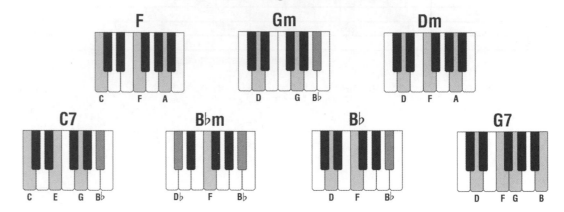

Music and Lyrics by Kristen Anderson-Lopez
and Robert Lopez

Happy Shuffle

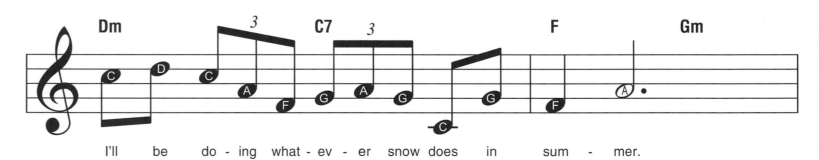

OLAF: Bees - 'll buzz, kids - 'll blow dan - de - li - on fuzz, and

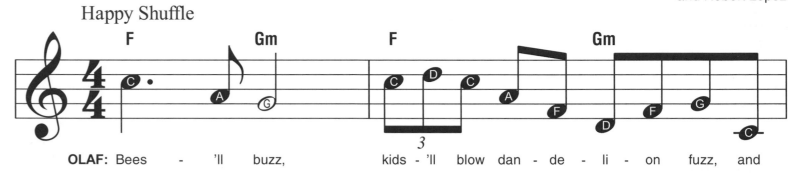

I'll be do - ing what - ev - er snow does in sum - mer.

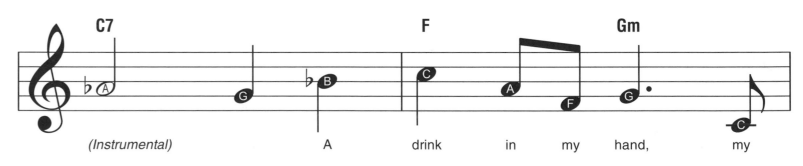

(Instrumental) A drink in my hand, my

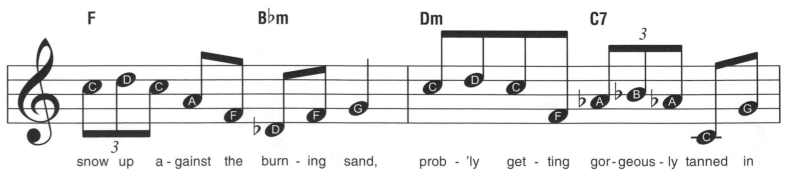

snow up a - gainst the burn - ing sand, prob - 'ly get - ting gor - geous - ly tanned in

15

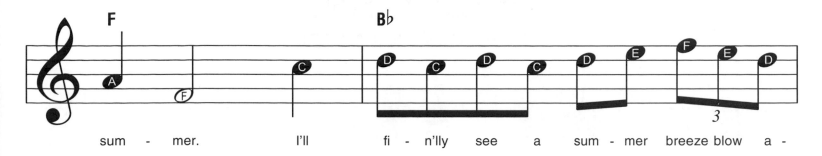

sum - mer.   I'll   fi - n'lly   see   a   sum - mer   breeze   blow   a -

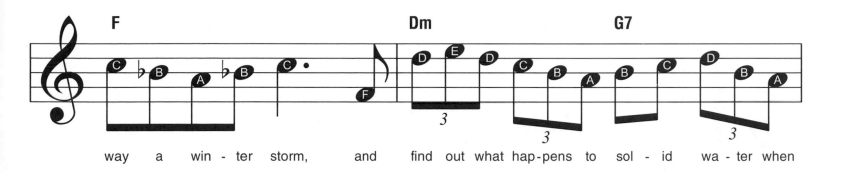

way   a   win - ter   storm,   and   find   out   what   hap-pens   to   sol - id   wa - ter   when

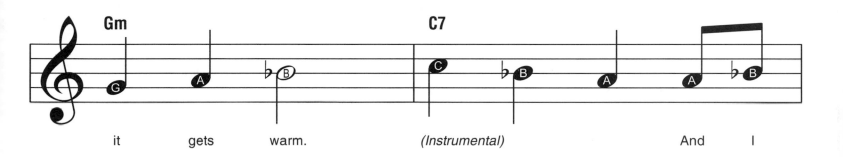

it   gets   warm.   (Instrumental)   And   I

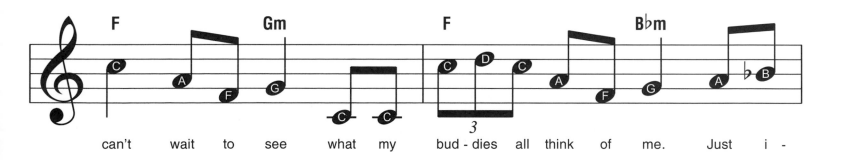

can't   wait   to   see   what   my   bud - dies   all   think   of   me.   Just   i -

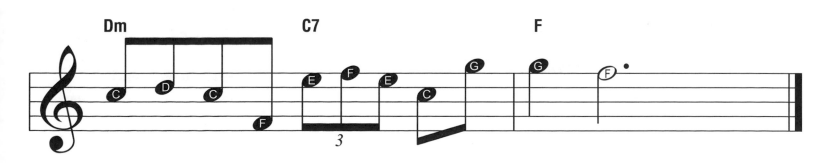

mag - ine   how   much   cool - er   I'll   be   in   sum - mer!

Fixer Upper
from Disney's *FROZEN*

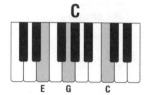

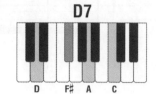

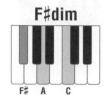

Music and Lyrics by Kristen Anderson-Lopez
and Robert Lopez

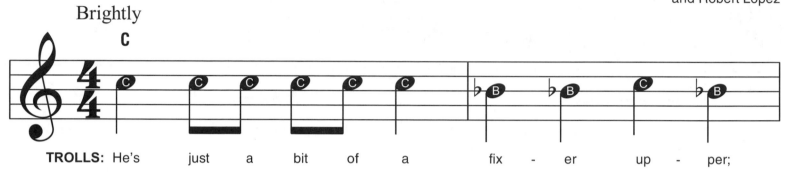

TROLLS: He's just a bit of a fix - er up - per;

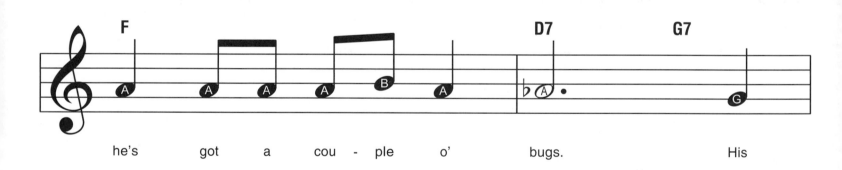

he's got a cou - ple o' bugs. His

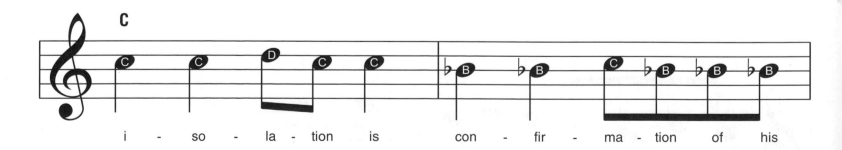

i - so - la - tion is con - fir - ma - tion of his

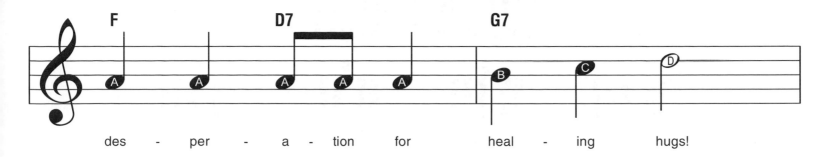

des - per - a - tion for heal - ing hugs!

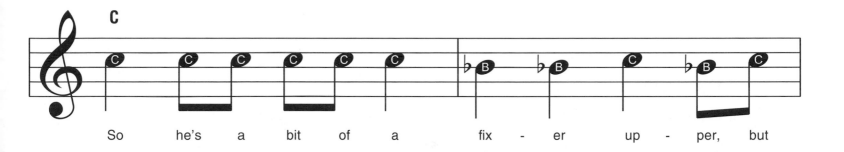

So he's a bit of a fix - er up - per, but

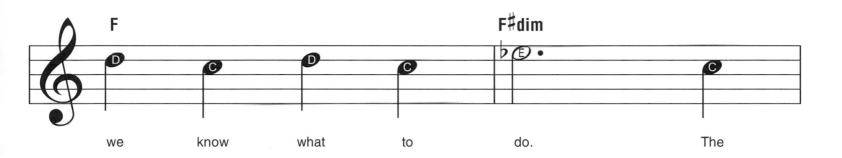

we know what to do. The

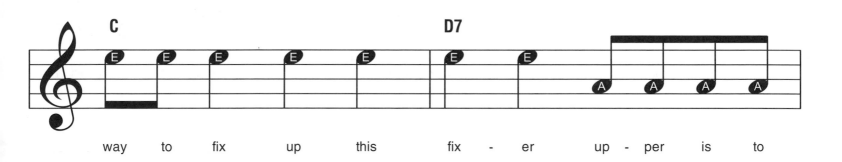

way to fix up this fix - er up - per is to

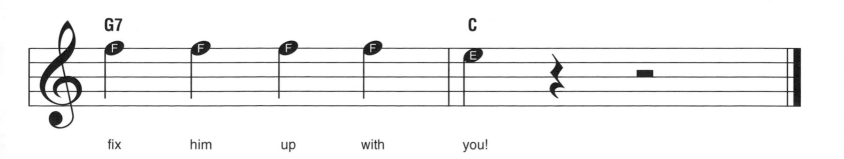

fix him up with you!

All Is Found
from Disney's *FROZEN 2*

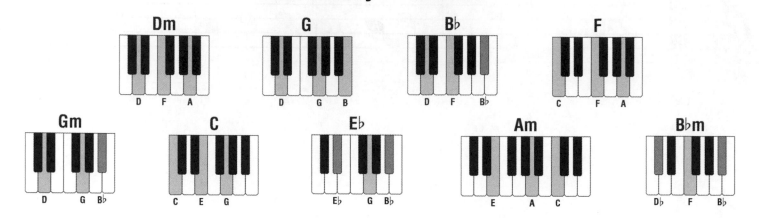

Music and Lyrics by Kristen Anderson-Lopez
and Robert Lopez

Moderately

QUEEN IDUNA:

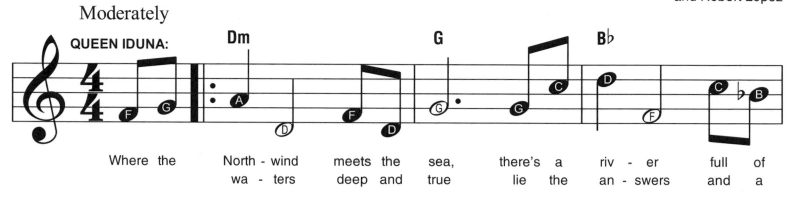

Where the North-wind meets the sea, there's a riv-er full of
wa-ters deep and true lie the an-swers and a

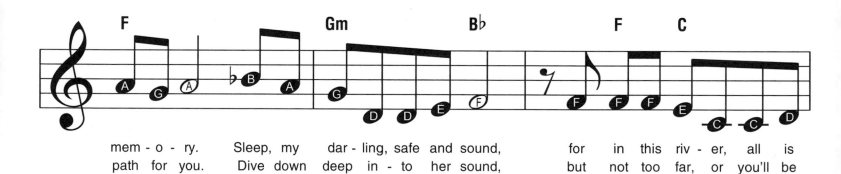

mem-o-ry. Sleep, my dar-ling, safe and sound, for in this riv-er, all is
path for you. Dive down deep in-to her sound, but not too far, or you'll be

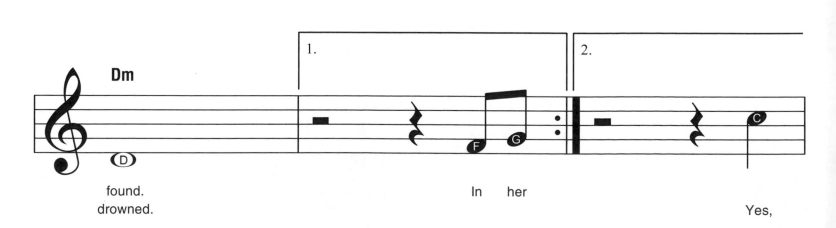

found.   In her
drowned.   Yes,

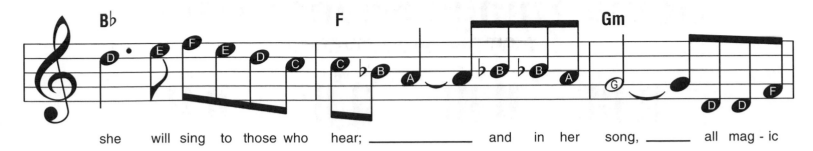

she will sing to those who hear; _____ and in her song, _____ all mag - ic

flows. _____ But can you brave what you most fear? Can you

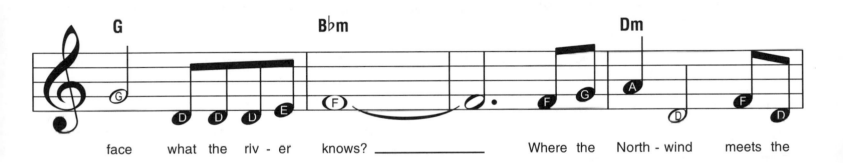

face what the riv - er knows? _____ Where the North - wind meets the

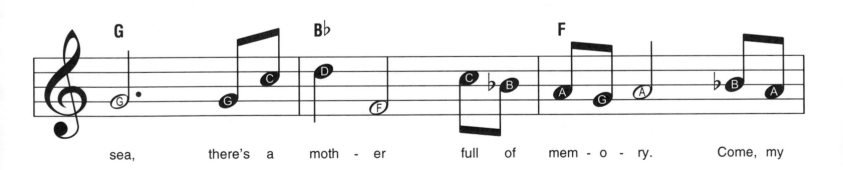

sea, there's a moth - er full of mem - o - ry. Come, my

dar - ling, home - ward bound. When all is lost, then all is found.

Some Things Never Change

from Disney's *FROZEN 2*

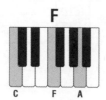
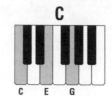
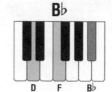

Music and Lyrics by Kristen Anderson-Lopez
and Robert Lopez

Rhythmically

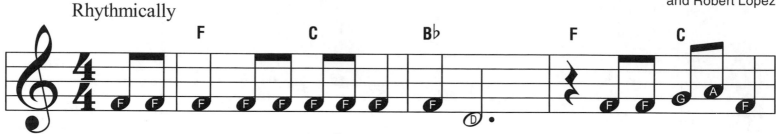

ANNA: Yes, the wind blows a lit - tle bit cold - er, and we're all get - ting

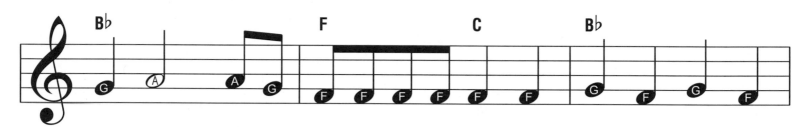

old - er. And the clouds are mov - ing on with ev - 'ry au - tumn

breeze. _____ Pe - ter Pump - kin just be - came fer - ti -

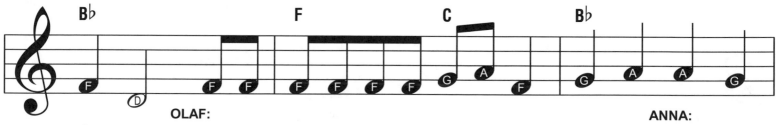

liz - er. **OLAF:** And my leaf's a lit - tle sad - der and wis - er. **ANNA:** That's why

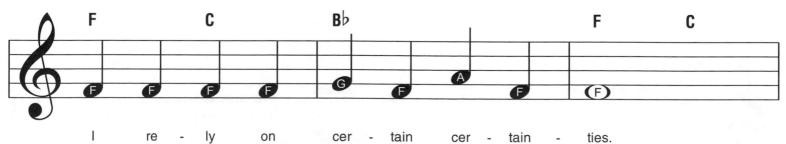

I re - ly on cer - tain cer - tain - ties.

Into the Unknown
from Disney's *FROZEN 2*

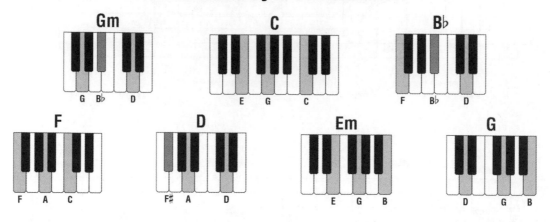

Music and Lyrics by Kristen Anderson-Lopez
and Robert Lopez

With determination

ELSA: You're not a voice; you're just a ring-ing in my ear. And if I heard you, *(which I don't)* I'm spo-ken for, I fear.

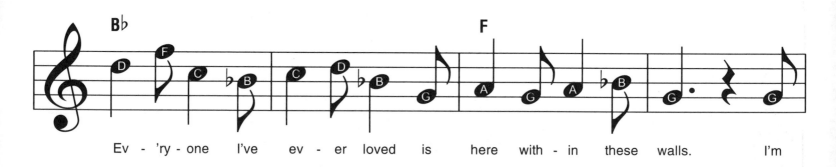

Ev-'ry-one I've ev-er loved is here with-in these walls. I'm sor-ry, se-cret si-ren, but I'm block-ing out your calls. I've

When I Am Older

from Disney's *FROZEN 2*

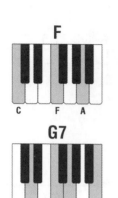
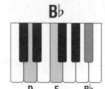

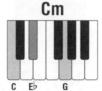
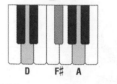
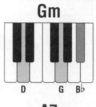
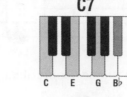
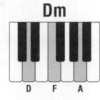
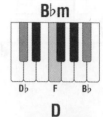

Music and Lyrics by Kristen Anderson-Lopez
and Robert Lopez

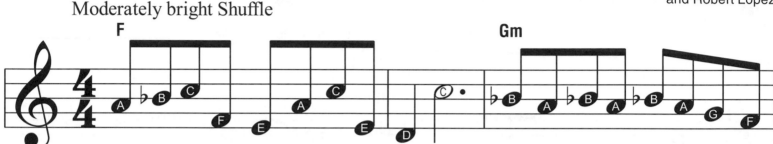

OLAF: This will all make sense when I am old-er. Some-day, I will see that this makes
that will all make sense when I am old-er. No need to be ter-ri-fied or

sense. One day, when I'm old and wise, I'll think back and re-al-ize that
tense. I'll just dream a-bout a time

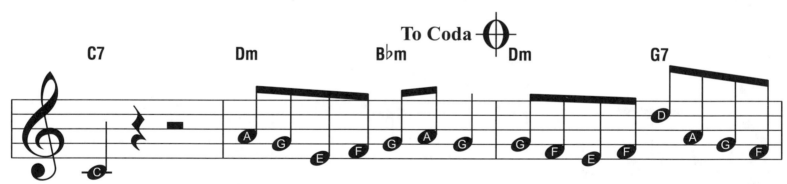

these were all com-plete-ly nor-mal e-vents! (Scream) I'll have all the an-swers when I'm

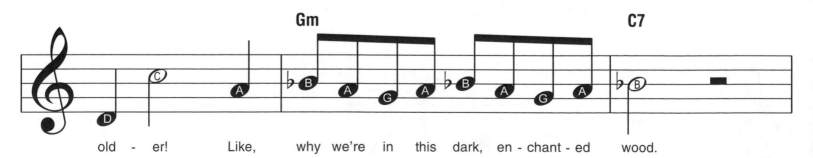

old-er! Like, why we're in this dark, en-chant-ed wood.

© 2019 Wonderland Music Company, Inc.
All Rights Reserved. Used by Permission.

Lost in the Woods
from Disney's *FROZEN 2*

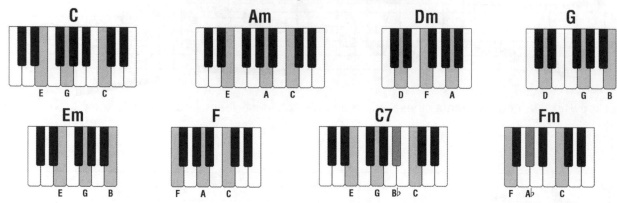

Music and Lyrics by Kristen Anderson-Lopez
and Robert Lopez

Moderate half-time feel

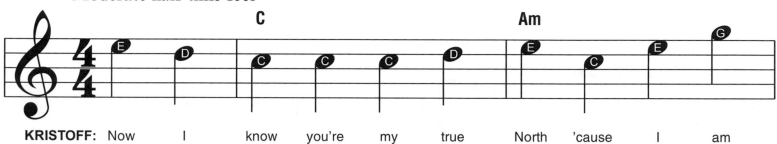

KRISTOFF: Now I know you're my true North 'cause I am

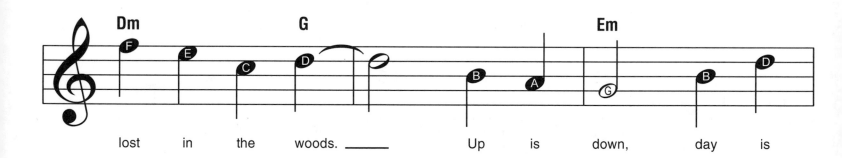

lost in the woods. _____ Up is down, day is

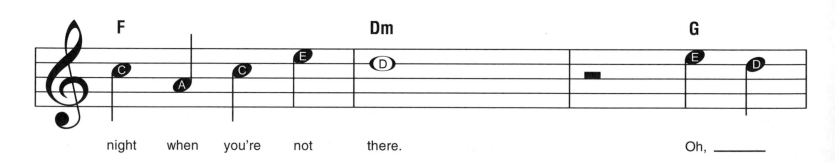

night when you're not there. Oh, _____

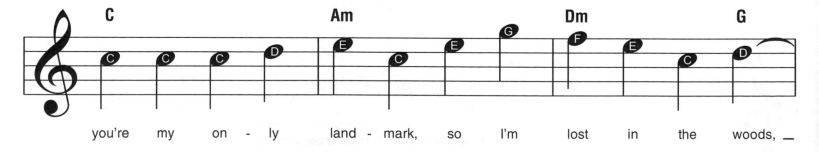

you're my on - ly land - mark, so I'm lost in the woods, _

© 2019 Wonderland Music Company, Inc.
All Rights Reserved. Used by Permission.

27

Show Yourself
from Disney's *FROZEN 2*

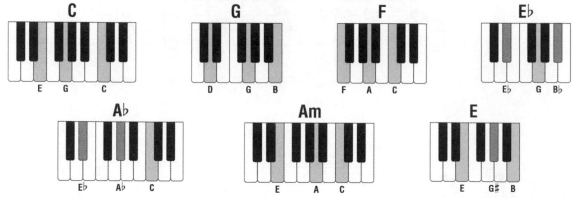

Music and Lyrics by Kristen Anderson-Lopez
and Robert Lopez

29

The Next Right Thing

from Disney's *FROZEN 2*

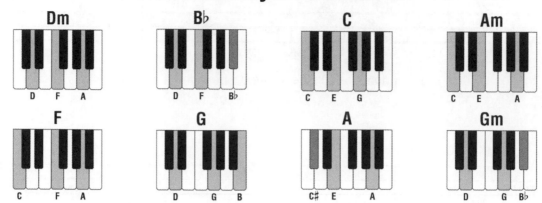

Music and Lyrics by Kristen Anderson-Lopez
and Robert Lopez

With emotion

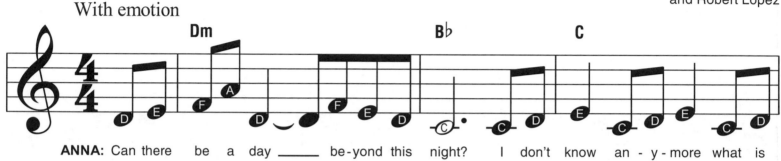

ANNA: Can there be a day ____ be-yond this night? I don't know an-y-more what is

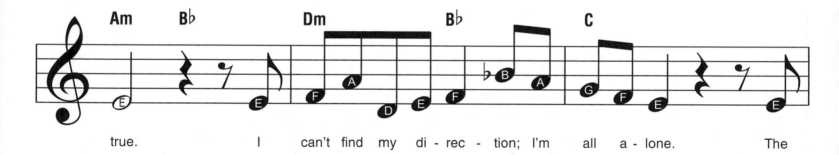

true.   I   can't find my di - rec - tion; I'm   all   a - lone.   The

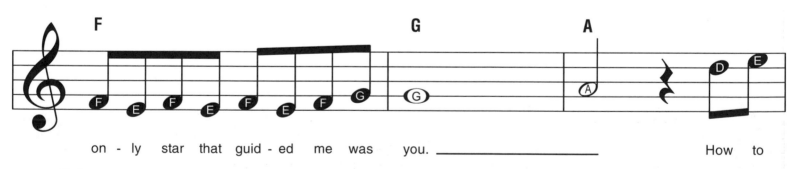

on - ly star that guid - ed   me was you. _____   How to

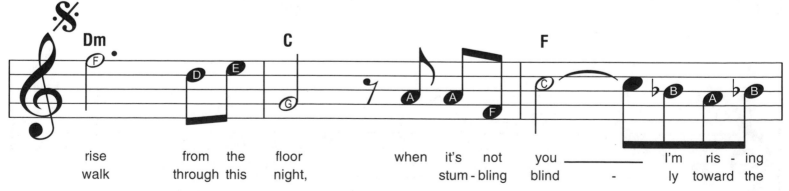

rise   from the   floor   when it's not   you _____ I'm ris - ing
walk   through this night,   stum - bling blind - ly toward the

SUPER EASY SONGBOOK

It's super easy! This series features accessible arrangements for piano, with simple right-hand melody, letter names inside each note, and basic left-hand chord diagrams. Perfect for players of all ages!

ADELE
00394705 22 songs.............................$14.99

THE BEATLES
00198161 60 songs.............................$15.99

BEAUTIFUL BALLADS
00385162 50 songs.............................$14.99

BEETHOVEN
00345533 21 selections.......................$9.99

BEST SONGS EVER
00329877 60 songs.............................$16.99

BROADWAY
00193871 60 songs.............................$15.99

JOHNNY CASH
00287524 20 songs.............................$9.99

CHART HITS
00380277 24 songs.............................$12.99

CHRISTMAS CAROLS
00277955 60 songs.............................$15.99

CHRISTMAS SONGS
00236850 60 songs.............................$15.99

CHRISTMAS SONGS WITH 3 CHORDS
00367423 30 songs.............................$10.99

CLASSIC ROCK
00287526 60 songs.............................$15.99

CLASSICAL
00194693 60 selections.......................$15.99

COUNTRY
00285257 60 songs.............................$15.99

DISNEY
00199558 60 songs.............................$15.99

BOB DYLAN
00364487 22 songs.............................$12.99

BILLIE EILISH
00346515 22 songs.............................$10.99

FOLKSONGS
00381031 60 songs.............................$15.99

FOUR CHORD SONGS
00249533 60 songs.............................$15.99

FROZEN COLLECTION
00334069 14 songs.............................$12.99

GEORGE GERSHWIN
00345536 22 songs.............................$9.99

GOSPEL
00285256 60 songs.............................$15.99

HIT SONGS
00194367 60 songs.............................$16.99

HYMNS
00194659 60 songs.............................$15.99

JAZZ STANDARDS
00233687 60 songs.............................$15.99

BILLY JOEL
00329996 22 songs.............................$11.99

ELTON JOHN
00298762 22 songs.............................$10.99

KIDS' SONGS
00198009 60 songs.............................$16.99

LEAN ON ME
00350593 22 songs.............................$10.99

THE LION KING
00303511 9 songs...............................$9.99

ANDREW LLOYD WEBBER
00249580 48 songs.............................$19.99

MOVIE SONGS
00233670 60 songs.............................$15.99

PEACEFUL MELODIES
00367880 60 songs.............................$16.99

POP SONGS FOR KIDS
00346809 60 songs.............................$16.99

POP STANDARDS
00233770 60 songs.............................$16.99

QUEEN
00294889 20 songs.............................$10.99

ED SHEERAN
00287525 20 songs.............................$9.99

SIMPLE SONGS
00329906 60 songs.............................$15.99

STAR WARS (EPISODES I-IX)
00345560 17 songs.............................$12.99

HARRY STYLES
01069721 15 songs.............................$12.99

TAYLOR SWIFT
1192568 30 songs..............................$14.99

THREE CHORD SONGS
00249664 60 songs.............................$16.99

TOP HITS
00300405 22 songs.............................$10.99

WORSHIP
00294871 60 songs.............................$16.99

HAL•LEONARD®

Prices, contents and availability subject to change without notice.

www.halleonard.com